The Path to Success
For Your Child

The Path to Success For Your Child

10 Easy to Follow Steps to Help Your Child Achieve Education Success

C. M. White

Gullah Girl Publishing
2015

The Path to Success for Your Child
10 Easy to Follow Steps to Help Your Child Achieve Education Success

First Printing: 2015

ISBN 978-0-9967540-0-2

Gullah Girl Publishing
www.GullahGirlPublishing.com

DISCLAIMER:
The purpose of this book is to educate and entertain. The author and publisher shall have neither liability nor responsibility for anyone with respect to any loss or damage caused, directly or indirectly, by the information contained in this book.

Individual results will vary. We cannot and do not make results guarantees or give professional or legal advice.

Ordering Information:
Special discounts are available on quantity purchases by corporations, associations, educators, and others. For details, contact the publisher at the above listed address.

U.S. trade bookstores and wholesalers: Please contact Gullah Girl Publishing
Email: GGPublishingCo@gmail.com.

DEDICATION

For all the parents and child advocates who do their very best to provide for our youth. Keep doing your best, learning from the mistakes, and fighting the good fight. You will never regret the time you spend providing children with their best opportunities.

Education is the most powerful weapon, which you can use to change the world – Nelson Mandela

TABLE OF CONTENTS

ACKNOWLEDGEMENTS

All things are possible through God. God gives me my purpose and the tools to accomplish that purpose. I am thankful.

Thank you to my parents, who taught me what it means to love and who encouraged me through every stage of my life. Thanks also to my brother, who has always been a best friend and continuous source of love for me.

Thanks to my two children who are a daily reminder of all that is right with the world. The two of you are amazing and will forever be loved. I love watching you find your way in this world and look forward to seeing just how you will make your mark on it.

And last, but not least - thank you to my husband and dedicated partner, who has shown me unconditional love. You believe in me and support all of my endeavors. You accept me for who I am - while encouraging me to be my best. You are my source of strength and peace.

Each of you has been an integral part in the birth of this book and I am very thankful.

FOREWARD

The Path to Success for Your Child has been a great resource. This book has challenged me to identify things about my child, my family, and goals for our future that I may have otherwise not examined so closely.

As a Family Nurse Practitioner and mother of two, my time is often limited; however, quality education for my children remains a high priority. *The Path to Success for Your Child*, is useful because it doesn't require large amounts of time to use. I can read it when I only have a few moments. When I'm done, I use the reflections section to jot down ideas and action steps to use until I get another moment to return to the book.

I recommend *The Path to Success for Your Child* to anyone needing direction on finding the best education for his or her child. Having this easy to follow guide, has taken the stress out of navigating the education system. Because of this book, I am on the right path to finding the best education opportunities for my children.

Alisha Orage,
MSN, APRN, FNP-C, MSRN

PREFACE

We're a military family at heart. We've spent over 20 years of our lives moving all over the world to serve our country. With each move, we faced the task of switching schools and settling into the norms of our new home. Each country, state, or city had different standards, expectations, and methods for education.

In the beginning, it was very difficult to adjust to those changes, but overtime things got easier. We developed a routine for conquering each move and adjusting to our new homes. Starting over never got easy, but it did get *easier*. It gave us the opportunity to learn that we were strong, resourceful, and resilient as individuals and as a family.

At each duty station, I usually worked at one of the local schools. I've held various positions in education such as substitute teacher, reading specialist, and math enrichment teacher. These positions all gave me a firsthand look at what works and doesn't work in education. I also saw that the differences in how schools approach to education could vary greatly. For example, some schools cared about overall student growth while others cared more about test scores.

Over the years, we were lucky to end up in great school districts. However, when we did find ourselves in a bad education environment, our years of experience had prepared us to handle it appropriately.

Without even realizing it, we had become semi-experts on how education works and what good education really looks like. We used that knowledge to identify the issues, fix those issues, or as a last resort, remove our kids from the school and find a situation that fit them better.

Throughout our numerous military moves, my children have attended private, public, online, and magnet schools, and have even been home schooled. We are open to any situation that results in a positive and successful education experience for them.

I embraced the idea that when it comes to education, we don't have to settle for what we're given. I learned that it was my job to give my children their best opportunity because that's what they deserved.

The more I learned about the world of education, the better equipped I felt to make good choices for my family. Protecting my children's education became a high priority. My children deserved teachers who cared about them individually and completely. They deserved schools that did more than just shuffle them through as a number or statistic.

In this book, I will share with you those valuable lessons I learned throughout our military journey. My hope is that by sharing my experiences, I can help others easily navigate education systems and identify the best education environment for their children.

Knowledge is the prime need of the hour
– Dr. Mary McLeod Bethune

INTRODUCTION

I'm sure you picked up this book because you care about your child's education. You may even have concerns about your child's current school. Maybe your concerns aren't serious. Maybe something just doesn't seem right. Whatever the reason, I'm glad you took an investigative step forward. By being proactive, you are changing the opportunities your child will have.

Education is not what is once was. The expectations, standards, culture, and variety of education options has opened the door for opportunity and confusion. With the introduction of the internet and other technological advances, we find a new set of education platforms to use. We aren't limited to a schoolhouse or other traditional methods for educating our children anymore. Understanding the various education options available is a huge part of ensuring success for our children.

Just as education has changed, so has parenting. It seems that parents are busier these days. Between providing for the family and keeping up with the activities of children parents find their time limited.

For example, many homes are comprised of parents who both work full time jobs and some homes have single parents working two jobs to make ends meet.

The makeup of the typical family has changed as well. There has been an increase of single parent homes and homes where grandparents are raising grandkids on their own.

These changes can leave little time to devote to the issue of quality education; however, quality education should always be a high priority. Without a quality education children are left struggling in a world they haven't been prepared to navigate. We must prepare them to be productive citizens for the future. Education is the key to that preparation. Although our time is often limited, finding quality education doesn't have to be a full time job.

By following the simple steps outlined in this book, you can put your child in the best environment for their individual success.

This easy to follow guide will take the guesswork out of the process and make getting your child a great education an attainable goal.

HOW TO USE THE BOOK

This book is broken into sections; *Steps* and *Reflections*.

Steps: Steps are simple rules that guide you towards finding the best education path for your child. These rules are things I've learned to apply as I searched for the best environment for my children. They are simple, but very effective.

Reflections: I have included pages at the end of each section where you can reflect on what you have learned. You can answer the questions I have posed or you can simply jot down your *light bulb* moments.

In your reflections, be sure to include ideas you'd like to research more, things you'd like to try, or observations you've already noticed. These will be great to come back to as you move forward in your education quest.

Remember this is simply a guide and foundation; a tool you can use to put your child on a path towards education success.

Think of others who might benefit from using this guide. Share it with them. While our own children are our greatest concern, we can all benefit from the success of one another. I want all children to succeed.

STEP 1

Get to Know Your Child

There's nothing more beautiful
Than acceptance for who you really are

Get to Know Your Child

Before you can give your child the best education opportunity, you must know your child. You may be thinking, "Of course I know my child. He/she is after all - *my* child." That would be an understandable response. For the sake of this lesson, try to forget what you know about your child. Try looking through the eyes of an unbiased observer.

By doing this, you may notice things you had not noticed before. Sometimes when we spend a large amount of time around a person, we miss some of the things that are unique about them. We instead focus on the norms, the things we have commonly grown to see.

I want you to look at your child as an individual because that's what they are. As parents, we often see our children as an extension of ourselves, but they are not. We are doing them a great disservice in not seeing them for whom they are and looking beyond the person, we've created.

I completely understand how difficult it can be to see *your baby* as their own person, but it is important that we approach it in this way. This gives us a chance to see who they truly are and separate what we *want* for them from what is ultimately *best* for them. You will come to find that those two things can differ greatly.

On the next few pages, you will look at your child's strengths, weaknesses, personality, and learning style. This is the first step in being able to choose the right educational options for your child.

STRENGTHS

Strengths are any skills, thinking, or behavior that allows a person to feel energized and empowered. Whatever enables your child to feel strong is a valid and important part of who they are.

Below you will find examples of characteristics that are considered strengths. Keep in mind that this list is subjective. Something one person considers a show of strength; another person might consider weakness. This is where taking stock in your families values comes into play. In the blank boxes, add characteristics that you consider your child's strengths.

Leader	Athletic	Intelligent	Artistic

WEAKNESSES

Weaknesses are any skills, thinking, or behavior that prevents a person from feeling energized and empowered. We all have them and most people lead productive lives with them. I embrace weaknesses because I think they make us the great people we are. However, with a little work most weaknesses can be overcome if necessary.

Below you will find examples of characteristics that are considered weaknesses. Again, this list is subjective. In the blank boxes, add characteristics that you consider weaknesses that might hinder learning in your child if not addressed or handled properly.

Stubborn	Talkative	Shy	Inattentive

PERSONALITY

Personality refers to characteristic patterns of thinking feeling, and behaving. I believe we learn to adapt our personalities to societal norms as we grow and mature. However, those basic traits still live within us. Understanding your child's personality helps you decide which environment will enhance and prepare them best to thrive in the world and in education.

Below you will find examples of personality traits. In the blank boxes, add traits that you believe personify your child.

Funny	Messy	Friendly	Lazy

LEARNING STYLE

Learning style is the way a person learns best. For example, some people learn best by doing, while others learn best by simply seeing something done. We each have our preferred learning styles. The outcome for success is much higher when we are taught using our preferred learning style.

Many schools have a one style fits all teaching style and don't consider that each student has their own way of learning. This often leads to some students being left out and not being able to fully grasp the ideas being taught.

On the next pages, you will find questions you can ask that will help determine your child's learning style. Your child may be able to help you with this. This list is not exhaustive; it is simply a beginning list of things to think about. You may think of other resources that will help find your child's learning style. There are tons of free online learning style tests that can further pinpoint your child's style.

FIND YOUR CHILD'S LEARNING STYLE

1. Does your child learn best by seeing how things work?

_____

_____

2. Does your child learn best by reading about how something works?

_____

_____

3. Does your child learn best by listening?

_____

_____

4. Does your child like to participate in discussions?

_____

_____

5. Does your child enjoy learning through physical activity?

_____

_____

6. Is your child logical or mathematical?

_____

_____

7. Is your child musical or artistic?

_____

_____

8. Does your child enjoy learning in groups?

_____

_____

8. Does your child like to work alone?

_____

_____

Remember to do an online search for learning style quizzes that will help further pinpoint your child's learning style.

REFLECTIONS:

How will understanding your child as an individual help you find the best education for them?

_____

_____

_____

_____

Other reflections:

_____

_____

_____

_____

_____

_____

_____

_____

_____

_____

_____

_____

_____

_____

STEP
2

Your Must Haves

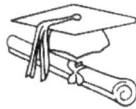

Intelligence plus character
That is the goal of true education

School Must Haves

What's important to one family may be completely irrelevant to another family and that's okay. The key for each of us is identifying what is important and necessary for *our* family. Step #1 helps with this process by helping you identify what your child needs. Identifying your child's needs will help you narrow down and pinpoint which specific criteria to look for in a school.

Every school puts emphasis on different things. Educating children should be the most important aspect of every school, but you'd be surprised to find that for some it isn't. It's up to us to research the different priorities of schools and put our children in the best position that will support their education success.

On the next pages, you will find a list of some of the most commonly sought after characteristics of schools. They are broken down into three categories: demographics, education, and culture. Getting a good educational experience for your child becomes much more attainable when these three categories are aligned with your family's needs and values.

DEMOGRAPHICS

Diversity - Students/staff who differ from one another based on gender, race, physical and mental abilities, class, etc. Are students learning to tolerate and work with people who are not like them?

Teacher - Student Ratio/Class size - The number of students assigned to each teacher. Are teachers overwhelmed? Are teachers able to give students individualized attention?

Location - Community/neighborhood, city school - Does everyone know one another or are they bussed from different areas? Community schools usually come with a family feel, while city schools tend to feel more institutional. Keep in mind that this is just a generalization and can vary from school to school.

Cost - Amount of money required to attend. While public schools are tuition free, there are still costs to attending them (field trips, technology fees, etc). Charter, Private, and Home Schools all have costs as well.

DEMOGRAPHICS (continued)

Average Income Levels - The amount of money families of students make. Are families able to contribute to fundraising efforts? Keep in mind that students of affluent families can be just as disruptive as students from less affluent families.

Teacher Turnover Rate - How long teachers stay at school. This can be an indication of how teachers are treated and whether they are happy in their jobs. When teachers are happy in their jobs, it's easier for them to focus on doing their jobs well.

EDUCATION

Pass/Fail/Graduation Ratios – This is one of many indications as to whether students are learning what is being taught. These ratios can depend on several factors. For example, student attendance can affect ratios because if students aren't at school to learn, then they most likely will fail. This shows that a school's pass/fail ratio, does not always give a clear picture of what's happening at the school.

Field Study - Going into the community and learning

firsthand how things work. In lower grades, this could be trips to museums and zoos. In upper grades, it could be a trip to a college.

Extra-Curricular - Academic clubs, athletic options such as Art, Future Farmers of America, Fellowship of Christian Athletes, Basketball, Football, etc.

Opportunities to explore - Internships and exposure to career fields help students decide what they want to pursue as a career.

Teaching Style – Teaching styles are just as varied as learning styles. Teaching styles range from hands-on teaching to lecture-style teaching to worksheet teaching.

Special Needs programs - Programs that support children with learning and/or physical disabilities.

Gifted/Accelerated programs - Programs that challenge students who have above average learning needs. These programs give students, who qualify, a chance to grow beyond the regular education classes.

Technology Use – Some schools depend heavily on technology for teaching, while others use little to none.

Some of the kinds of technology used in schools are tablets, laptops/notebooks, and interactive Smart Boards.

College Courses - Many schools have begun to collaborate with local colleges to offer college courses to students. Some students can even graduate from high school with an associate's degree.

Specialized training - Students take courses that result in certifications such as Microsoft Certification, Apple Developer Certification, HVAC certification, Nursing, and Cosmetology.

Magnet programs - These specialized courses or curricula are focused on a particular theme such as STEM (Science, Technology, Engineering, and Mathematics) and CTE (Career and Technical Education). Magnet refers to the way schools draw in students who may live out of the school zone.

CULTURE

Convenience - Things such as the distance to the school from your home, the availability of transportation, and the availability of before and after school care all contribute to the convenience of the school for your family's needs.

Religion - Some schools are religion based. Students may be required to take religious courses, attend religious events, or worship during school hours.

Discipline Procedures - Some of these include no tolerance policies on things like drugs, fighting, or weapons, expulsion, in-school suspension, afterschool detention, lunch detentions, a call to parents, and community service. It's important to know the laws that govern these procedures.

History - Some schools are hundreds of years old and have a history buried deep into the community while others are new and its history is just being constructed.

School Spirit - School Spirit can add to the fun of the school. It makes the students, staff, and community feel connected to a school and take pride in its upkeep.

Caring Teachers - Some teachers do the bare minimum of their job and see teaching as just a job, while others go above and beyond. Caring teachers are emotionally attached to their students and care about their students' success in and out of the classroom.

Community/City School - A community that rallies around the school to support events, fundraisers, and students helps make the school a success.

Safety/Security - Safety in schools is a real concern for many. Many schools have school resource officers (SRO) protect the student and staff. These SROs may be armed or unarmed. Many schools keep all doors locked aside from a single point of entry that is monitored at all times during school hours.

Uniforms - Schools have turned to uniforms to reduce the cost of clothing for parents, reduce students' focus on the latest fads, and level the playing field for families who may not have money to keep up with the latest fads.

These are just a sample of school characteristics. Think of others you find important and add them to your list of priorities. The main takeaway is that you must first identify what you're looking for so you can effectively find the school that fits your family's needs.

REFLECTIONS:

What is the most important characteristic you look for in a school?

_____

_____

_____

_____

Other reflections:

_____

_____

_____

_____

_____

_____

_____

_____

_____

_____

_____

_____

_____

Other reflections:

_____
_____
_____
_____
_____
_____
_____
_____
_____
_____
_____
_____
_____
_____
_____
_____
_____
_____
_____
_____
_____
_____
_____
_____
_____
_____
_____
_____
_____
_____

STEP
3

You Have Options

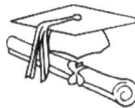

If a child can't learn the way we teach,
Maybe we should teach the way they learn.

You Have Options

We live in a time where education options are rapidly expanding, which means we no longer have to settle for whatever we are given. Instead, we can learn more about those options and find what works best for our families.

As the education system evolves and parents become more informed, other education options have become more prevalent and widely accepted. The most well-known options for education today are Public, Charter, Magnet, Private, Online, and Home school.

On the next pages, you will learn more about these options and use that knowledge to choose the best option for your family. You will find a brief description of education options, their costs, and pros and cons of each.

Whether something is a con or pro depends on your needs as a family. For example, homeschooling requires children and parents to be in the same vicinity for days at a time. Some parents cherish that time with their children and some parents are driven crazy if their kids are not out of the house.

Again, this is perfect example of why it's important to choose the education option that will work best for *your family's needs.*

Regardless of your choice, the important thing is to

understand what is available and the consequences of that choice. Through research and reading books such as this, you are becoming an educated advocate for your child.

PUBLIC SCHOOL

Public schools are schools that are maintained at public expense for the education of the children of a community or district. Public schools are part of a system of free public education commonly including primary and secondary schools.

Funded by: Tax Revenues from federal, state and local governments

Pros:
- Bus Transportation
- Teachers certified as required by state
- School accountable to a higher authority
- Low to no cost

Cons:
- Some schools underfunded
- Classrooms are often filled to capacity
- Standardized testing
- Learning is often not individualized

CHARTER SCHOOLS

Charter schools are self-ruling public schools created by a contract between a sponsor, such as a local school district or corporation, and an organizer, such as a group of teachers or a community group. The curriculum or focus of the school is often not traditional.

The key differences between charter schools and regular public schools lies in three elements that help define them: they are held accountable, not just in general, but to achievement goals embedded in their charters. Their student body is made up of children whose parents chose the school, and the school is tailored to the student body's needs. They are given freedom from certain bureaucratic procedures with the idea that this will give them a greater ability to focus on creating academic emphasis.

Funded by: Tax Revenues from federal, state and local governments

Pros:
- Often outperform their traditional public school counterparts
- Funded based on student enrollment so they work hard to appease families by offering great programs

- School accountable to a higher authority
- Low to no cost

Cons:
- Some schools underfunded
- Parents are often responsible for transportation
- Not always constrained by state laws requiring teaching credentials
- Not approved in all states

MAGNET SCHOOLS

Magnet schools are also a kind of public school or program. A magnet school may provide a focus, whether academic or social, on a special theme.

Funded by: Federal, state, and local taxes
Pros:
- More choice in curriculum

- Builds community relationships for both parent and student
- Access to sports programs
- Access to arts and music programs
- Teachers are certified educational instructors.

- Low cost

Cons:
- Larger class sizes
- Exposure to unacceptable lifestyles at public schools
- Classes are taught at a mid-learning level, which may cause advanced learners to become bored
- Limited access to learning materials

PRIVATE SCHOOLS

Private schools are founded, conducted, and maintained by a private group rather than by the government, usually charging tuition and often following a particular philosophy, viewpoint, etc.

Funded by: Tuition, endowments

Pros:
- Smaller class sizes
- Private schools have better books and supplies
- More access to up-to-date computers
- Curriculum is more challenging
- Most private schools are religious based schools

Cons:

- Cost
- Teachers are not required to have a teaching degree, just knowledge of the subject they will be teaching
- Less diverse choices in subjects
- Often no special education classes available
- Students must pass an entrance exam to be admitted
- Most private schools are religious based schools

HOME SCHOOL

Simply put, homeschooling is teaching your child at home instead of sending them off to school.

Funded by: Parents

Pros:
- Free to choose curriculum
- Free to choose schedule
- Small teacher to student ratio
- Teaches students to be independent in their learning choices

Cons:
- Usually more expensive than public school
- Teachers are not always qualified to teach all subjects

- Can be harder to provide social interaction
- Colleges sometimes have stricter admission policies concerning homeschooled students.

ONLINE SCHOOL

Public and private schools offer online learning opportunities. Students can attend a traditional school, while taking supplemental online courses or they can withdraw from traditional school and take only online courses.

Funded By: Varies based on program

Pros:
- Self-paced
- Flexible Schedule
- Curriculum choices

Cons:
- Self-discipline required
- Lack of human interaction

REFLECTIONS:

Which option or combination of options do you think would work best for your child?

_____

_____

_____

_____

Why do you think those options would work best for your child?

_____

_____

_____

_____

_____

_____

_____

_____

_____

_____

_____

_____

_____

STEP
4

Use Your Resources

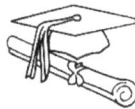

---

*Don't sit and wait for opportunities to come,
Get up and make them.*

Use Your Resources

There are many resources available to help you find the best education options in your area. Sometimes you have to dig. I've learned that oftentimes, you have to revisit a resource to get the full story. You may run into people who don't know the information or simply aren't willing to share it with you. Returning on another day, at another time, may give you a chance to speak with someone else who is more knowledgeable and/or forthcoming.

An example of this is when I was in search of a medical program for my child. First, I called my child's school for information. The guidance counselor said the program was unavailable. When I inquired about when it might become available, she told me she didn't know anything except that it wasn't available at that time. She was as helpful as she knew how to be, but was far from what I expected from a school official.

I was a little discouraged, but because the program was important to my child, I didn't accept that the counselor's answer as the end of the road. Instead, it was just a roadblock. I decided I would have to take a detour to avoid it.

I wasn't sure what my next step would be, but after a lot of thought, I called another local school to inquire about the program. Yes, even though it wasn't my child's school, I called anyway. The school was on the same grade level as my child so I thought maybe they offered the program and would possibly know something about it. It didn't hurt to try. The worse that could happen is they would think I was a crazy person, but the best that could happen is that I might just find the information I needed. For me, it was worth taking the chance.

The first call, the guidance counselor was very nice. She confirmed that the school did offer the program and connected me to the teacher who taught the program. The teacher was in the middle of class so I had to leave a message. I left my name, number and the program I was calling about. After a few days of no return call, I called again and had to leave another message. Hey, this was for my child. There is nothing more important.

That afternoon, I got a call from the teacher who taught the program at the school. I explained to her that my child attended a different school, but was interested in the program and having trouble getting information. She was very understanding and happy to help. She had tons of details about the program, which was very much available at my child's school. She even offered information about other programs I might want to look into. She was knowledgeable and willing to help.

I was happy that I didn't give up at that first road block. Because of that, I was able to connect with a great educator who I am great friends with even to this day. My child was able to enroll in the program and graduated as a certified Pharmacy Technician because of it!

The point is that finding information can sometimes be a frustrating journey, but when you consider your reasons for embarking, you find yourself with a strong resolve to continue.

On the next pages, I've listed Five Easy Steps I take in gathering information. I've also listed Starting Point Resources that have proved to be successful for finding information about schools and programs. Be warned! Some may think you're a little crazy for asking so many questions, but you just keep moving full steam ahead as a strong advocate for your child.

FIVE EASY STEPS FOR GETTING THE INFORMATION YOU NEED

STEP ONE: Identify the programs, schools, or activities you're interested in.

STEP TWO: Write down the email addresses, phone numbers, and addresses for the contact person listed for the business.

STEP THREE: Call and ask for details. If no answer, send an email, and if no luck with either and you're really interested, stop by.

STEP FOUR: If whomever you corresponded with in STEP THREE wasn't forth coming with information, start over at STEP TWO to find any alternative contact information and repeat STEP FOUR using the alternative information.

STEP FIVE: Continue to follow the steps until you get the information you need!

STARTING POINT RESOURCES

Internet - The first stop is the internet! Enter the activity, program, or school into the search engine along with location and sit back as the information essentially, comes to you.

Review Sites - Sites such as SchoolDigger.com and GreatSchools.org are great resources for information. There you can find school grade reports, statistics such as diversity and teacher to student ratios. If you're in the market for a new home, Great Schools has a tool for researching which schools are zoned for which neighborhoods. Of course you must verify *Great Schools* information with the school district before actually purchasing the home.

Websites - Most programs, activities, and schools have a presence on the Internet. It's a great starting point for finding out directly from them what they offer. I always make note of any pictures they share for an idea of whom they are trying to impress and who is included in their posts.

Social Media - Check out their Twitter, Facebook and other social media pages as well to see what kinds of information they share. Are they engrained into the community? Are their values aligned with yours? These are all things you can get a feel for through what's posted online. Social media often gets a bad rap, but it all depends on how you use it. It can be very useful in getting behind the scenes information and connecting with like-minded people.

Books - You are already on the right track because you picked up this one! Books usually contain some of what you already know combined with new insights. All of this is then compiled into an easy to follow action plan. That makes getting organized less stressful and helps keep you on track.

A money-saving tip is to use your local library to peruse books. That way you get to try before you buy. When it comes navigating the education system, you need to be an expert to some degree. The more you read about it, the more knowledgeable and empowered you will be to make good decisions for your children.

Parents - One of my family's challenges has been moving to new places and knowing no one. We didn't have friends or family to go to for information. That coupled with me not really being a social butterfly posed quite a challenge. As I watched my children grow and navigate new schools, new rules, new cultures, I realized it was imperative that I do the same.

I quickly learned to reach out to new people because my

need for information became more powerful than my nervousness to talk to people I didn't know.

When seeking information from people, be sure to do so cautiously. One person's version of a "good school" may not be your definition of a "good school". Get specific information about why they feel how they feel about the school. Weigh that against what you are looking for in a school for your child. Remember, even if your family's values differ from those you talk to, you can still gain valuable information from them on how to navigate the different activities, programs, and schools available in the area.

REFLECTIONS:

What resources have you used in the past to attain information?

_____

_____

_____

_____

How could building a network of resources be helpful for you?

_____

_____

_____

_____

_____

_____

_____

_____

_____

_____

_____

_____

Other reflections:

STEP
5

Get Connected

Coming together is the beginning. Keeping together is progress. Working together is success.

Get Connected

Once you've chosen the school, activity, or program, you're interested in, the work towards success continues. This step focuses on connecting with the programs you have chosen.

I've heard teachers say they've reached out to parents to help a student, but got no response from the parent. Some teachers have gone as far as visiting homes only to have parents not answer the door or rudely turn them away. The mere fact that you're reading this book says you're not that kind of parent.

When it comes to a child's success in school, a parent's involvement is just as important as the school itself. Most good schools have implemented various communication tools that make it easy to foster a positive relationship between school and home.

Note for those who choose to home school: Being connected requires you to reach out to local home school organizations. Each state has its own laws on homeschooling. Use the resources suggested in STEP 4 to find the agencies, organizations, and parents who can point you in the right direction. You will need them as you begin and throughout your home schooling journey.

Email: The consensus among most teachers polled is that email is the most convenient way to communicate between home and school. Teachers can email at their leisure and parents can respond at their leisure. A drawback is the interpretation of the email. Sometimes the intent of the email is misconstrued or misunderstood which could further compound issues. When dealing with sensitive issues like grades or behavior, it's best to try other methods of communication that allow for immediate response and effective communication.

Telephone: Reaching a teacher by telephone is not an easy task. They have long days in the classroom and don't always get a chance to check messages and return calls. If something is pressing, it's probably best to email first and ask the teacher to give you a call.

Text Alerts: In this age of smartphones and other technologies, text alerts have made their way into the school system. Many schools use text alerts to keep parent abreast of any changes to schedules or upcoming events. Some systems require parents to subscribe; others are built from a database of current parents of students enrolled. These alerts are an easy way for schools to get information out quickly to a large number of people.

Newsletters: Newsletters are a great way for the school to keep parents informed about the happenings at the school. Some schools do one newsletter for the entire school, others have newsletters for each grade level, and some have individual teachers produce their own classroom newsletters. As students get into higher-grade levels, parents and teachers find that the newsletters don't make it home as often as they should. For this reason, many schools have turned to producing online newsletters that can be accessed anytime.

Blog/Website: Similar to a newsletter, blogs are online records of the happenings in the school. Schools can include pictures, calendars, and a wide variety of other information on the blog/website. Parents can subscribe to the blog to get updates delivered directly to their emails.

Powerschool: Powerschool is a program that many schools use. It is a window into your child's education. Parents can use Powerschool to keep track of:

- Grades for current classes, as well as the assignments that make up those grades
- Attendance for the past two weeks, quarter, or the entire school year including a legend of attendance codes used by the school

- Teacher comments
- Discipline Logs
- Reports via Email - allows parents to request daily, weekly, or monthly reports to be sent via email
- Daily School Bulletin

Powerschool is a great way to stay on top of grades, attendance, events, and discipline and to catch any issues before they become irreversible. Powerschool is just one of the brands of software available to schools use a resource for parents.

Conferences: I can't imagine the traditional parent teacher conference ever being replaced. Some conferences now include parents, teachers, lead teachers, and principals. This is to ensure there are many voices available to offer support for the student. This also helps to protect all involved should something said during the conference comes into dispute later.

There is nothing quite as effective as sitting down face to face and coming to an understanding on the status of your child's education. It's good for the people most invested in a child's education to get to know one another's intentions and come together in the best interest of the child.

REFLECTIONS:

What is your preferred way to stay connected to your child's teacher and school?

_____

_____

_____

_____

What other ways might you try to stay connected to your child's teacher and school?

_____

_____

_____

_____

_____

_____

_____

_____

_____

_____

_____

_____

_____

_____

Other reflections:

_____

_____

_____

_____

_____

_____

_____

_____

_____

_____

_____

_____

_____

_____

_____

_____

_____

_____

_____

_____

_____

_____

STEP
6

Stay Informed

I've learned that I still have a lot to learn.

Stay Informed

Once you've recorded the emails and phone numbers and subscribed to newsletters and blogs you're ready to use those things to stay informed.

Some parents say things like "that's the teacher's job" or "they don't need to call me so much. They need to handle it because that's what I send the kids to school for." That couldn't be further from the truth. Educating children is a partnership between home, school, and community. It literally takes a village to ensure our children are educated properly. The first and most important people in that village are the parents.

It's the parent's job to stay plugged into what's happening with our children. We are the ones who should strive to identify changes or issues and work to handle them; with the help of schools and community if needed. We should be the first ones to celebrate encourage, and reward out children as they learn and grow.

Of course, all of this requires parents to have relationship with the school. Parents need the school to keep a watchful eye, especially since our children spend most of their waking hours at school.

Still, it all comes down to parental responsibility. If a school is not providing what our children need, it is our duty to find other options for them. Those options may be as simple as free/paid tutoring with the child's teacher or an after school program. It may be as complex as a move to another school. One effective way for parents to know if the school is providing what their child needs is by staying informed.

I've found it important to be informed in these three major areas at all times: Assignments, Assessments, and Social Learning.

Assignments:

Assignments are given to give a student practice on a subject the teacher has taught or is preparing to teach. Teachers usually have a website, newsletter, or some way for parents to know what the assignments are.

While it's first your child's responsibility to stay on top of their assignments, you have to stay on top of the assignments as well. Knowing your child's assignments helps you if your child is not progressing, as they should. You will be able to pinpoint if the progress is due to missed assignments or some other issue.

As mentioned previously, some schools also have online programs such as Powerschool that allows you to log in and see your child's assignments and grades. If your child's school doesn't have this, you can request grades on a weekly basis to stay on top of things.

Some things you might want to keep track of are: What is your child being taught? What curriculum is being used? Is it on track with national standards? What are the assignments being given? How often? Is your child turning in assignments?

Assessments:

Assessments are given to gauge how much of a lesson the student has mastered. Students are given several assessments; quizzes, monthly tests, and state or national standardized tests. Testing can be daunting and tiring for students. They need support and encouragement to study. Being informed helps parents know when assessments are taking place so they can be the support their student needs.

Social Learning:

Social learning is just as important as academic learning. Many messages are being thrown at our children in school. They are seeing things that don't always agree with what we are teaching them at home. Parents have to stay on top of what messages their student is receiving to ensure that positive messages outweigh the negative ones.

An informed parent should know things about the school like: What's the discipline policy? Are students behaving poorly with no consequence? What messages are being thrown at your child? If you don't know you can't combat those messages?

While children will be exposed to many different ideas and values, if we teach them our values and support them when they make good choices, we can help steer them in the right direction.

Note for home school families:

Since you are your child's teacher, you are already plugged into what's going on with assignments, assessments, and social learning. However, there are some instances where you may not be the teacher.

For instance, you may choose to use outside sources in your child's education such as cooperative teaching, supplemental activities, or part-time enrollment in programs at the local school. Cooperative teaching is where parents allow other parents to teach their students in a subject they may not feel comfortable teaching. Supplemental activities are things like music lessons and recreational sports. Enrollment in sports at the local school your child is zoned for became possible in some states. All of these instances create a situation where you won't always have insight into what's happening with your child. Using the resources in STEP #5 will help you stay in touch with your child's accomplishments in those kinds of programs.

REFLECTIONS:

How do you think staying informed could help your child?

_____

_____

_____

_____

What are some of the ways you stay informed about Assignments, Assessments, and Social Learning? :

_____

_____

_____

_____

_____

_____

_____

_____

_____

_____

_____

_____

_____

_____

_____

STEP
7

Stay Engaged

A child educated only at school,
Is an uneducated child

72

Stay Engaged

Staying engaged is similar to staying informed, but the focus is on staying engaged with your child. While we have hopes and dreams for our children, we must remember that this life is *with our guidance* their own.

Their life must be something they are happy with. When what they think matters to us, our children find it easier to be confident in sharing what they think with others.

Although we've been where they are to some degree, times do and have changed. Our children are faced with a fast paced, high technology world. They have to quickly learn how to navigate our rapidly changing world.

It takes us being open to their views and allowing them to share their thoughts without judgment for us to have a close connection with them. They need a safe place to bring their concerns and embarrassing situations. If you can be that safe place, you will most likely be plugged in to what's going on with your child because they will tell you themselves.

Children are all different, some will come home ready to share every aspect of their day with parents, and others are more reserved and will barely share even when asked. We have to engage with our children. Take interest in what's important to them. When we show interest in their interest, they tend to open up and share more.

I've listed some things that may help you plug into your child's point of view.

Child's perceptions of school

- Are the teachers friendly and approachable?
- Are the Principals friendly and approachable?
- Do school leaders follow through on promises?
- Is discipline addressed equally and fairly?
- Does your child feel safe at school?
- Are the assignments too easy/too hard?
- Does the school offer extra-curricular activities your child is interested in?
- Is your child enjoying their classes?

Social environment (who they hang out with)

- Is your child comfortable being themselves at the school?
- Does your child feel accepted for who they are?
- What kinds of peer pressures is your child facing?
- Latest fads
- Dating

Goals: What they want and are working towards

- What are the goals your child has set for themselves?
- Why are these goals important to them?
- How does your child plan to achieve these goals?
- Is anyone helping them achieve these goals?
- What roadblocks have they faced?
- What successes have they achieved?

Dreams: What they want, but haven't yet begun working towards

- What are their dreams?
- Why do they think these dreams would be good for them?
- Who do they see sharing in those dreams with them?
- When do they plan to turn their dreams into goals and begin work towards achieving those goals?

REFLECTIONS:

What can you do to become more engaged with your child?

_____

_____

_____

_____

Other reflections:

_____

_____

_____

_____

_____

_____

_____

_____

_____

_____

_____

_____

_____

_____

Other reflections:

STEP
8

Hold them Accountable

I can accept failure - everyone fails at something
But I can't accept not even trying.

Hold Them Accountable

Many people have a role to play in your child achieving a quality education. As you've probably figured out, I believe the most important factor in a child's education are parents. While that doesn't require parents to know everything or have a PhD in Education, it does require that parents put energy into finding and learning from people who do have that much needed knowledge.

STEP #8 is holding the people accountable who have the highest stake in your child's education. Whether you're a home school parent, a traditional school parent, or even an online school parent, you will be pointing the finger at yourself first, then your child, your supporting family, and the community of people you have chosen to supplement your child's education.

Holding them accountable means just that. Requiring that they do the part, they have signed up to do. This doesn't require an ugly confrontation or battle, but it does sometimes require a conversation and a watchful eye. Always try to keep it positive. Make sure that the interests of your child is the focus. Choose your words wisely, try not to place blame. Instead, always look for solutions.

Below I've listed some of the responsibilities potentially major stakeholders in your child's education are accountable for. This list is not exhaustive. You may have more, less or different responsibilities assigned to your major players.

Your Child
- Schoolwork - studying, completing, staying up to date
- Behavior - paying attention in class, following school rules
- Communicating - needs for help with schoolwork, social situations, etc.
- Good social decisions - choosing appropriate friends, following rules, taking care of oneself, making choices that align with family values

Teachers
- Teaching - making sure each student grasps the material, preparing students for tests
- Guidance - keeping a watchful eye out for student issues/social problems and positive actions
- Communication - letting the parent know what's going on in the classroom with their child. (problems and positives)
- Safety - keeping students safe by removing problems from class or reporting them to administrators

- Leading- setting an example for students of positive behavior, treating all students fairly and equally

Administrators
- Safety - keeping students safe from insiders and outsiders
- Communication - keeping parents updated on latest school happenings such as staff changes, new rules/standards, issues at the school, and discipline issues
- Guidance - keeping an open door policy and encouraging students to come to them with any problems so they can help the student
- Leading - setting an example of positive behavior and treating all students equally and fairly
- Supporting - Supporting teacher, parent, student relationships to allow for excellence in learning

Parents
- Guidance - being open and listening to your child in order to help the child navigate positively through society and school
- Supportive - Helping child with homework, schoolwork, social situations even when that means enlisting help, reward accomplishments

- Leading - setting an example of positive behavior that the child can learn from
- Be Informed - know what's going on with all the major players of your child's education
- Be Engaged - using your connections to stay actively engaged in your child's life and education
- HOLD THEM ACCOUNTABLE

REFLECTIONS:

Why do you think the list of responsibilities for parents is longer than any other stakeholder?

_____

_____

_____

_____

Other reflections:

_____

_____

_____

_____

_____

_____

_____

_____

_____

_____

_____

_____

_____

STEP

9

Stay Active

Nothing will work...unless you do

Stay Active

Educating students is not an easy task. Many moving parts must be maintained and monitored for things to go well. A great way parents can help with that is to stay active in the school. Most schools have organizations that help teachers, enhance learning, and offer fun activities for students; PTO, PTSA, and SIC are just a few of them.

Staying active at your child's school gives you a chance to get to know the people who play a major role in your child's education. It helps build relationships. Relationships are important for several reasons. Relationships ensure that we don't live or work in isolation. It gives us a community of people to turn to for help or when we want to celebrate.

Building positive relationships with the major stakeholders in your child's education gives you a circle to turn for help and a circle of people who like you, are cheering your child on to success. Sometimes it's difficult to build those relationships, especially if the school is close-knit or full of cliques. While those can be barriers, they don't mean defeat.

Joining parent groups, volunteering, donating to fundraisers, and attending school events are all great ways to get your foot in the door and begin to build those very important relationships.

Below I've listed some of the most common parent organizations, your school, online school, or home school may have more, less, or different programs. Use your resources to find out what's offered in your area.

PTO/PTSA
PTO - Parent Teacher Organization
PTSA - Parent Teacher Student Association
PTA - Parent Teacher Association

These are three of the most nationally recognized parent groups. They are governed by national and local rules. These collaborative groups usually meet monthly and work throughout the year to bridge the gap between parents, teachers, community and school.

SIC - School Improvement Council

This group works to ensure the school is constantly improving academically and socially. The group comprised of teachers, parents, community leaders, and students looks for areas that need improvement and does the work to make those improvements happen.

Booster Club

These are support groups for sports, drama clubs, and other extra-curricular activities. They raise money, keep things organized, and support the participants in their respective activity. Booster clubs usually do fundraisers to help raise money for props, trips, food, uniforms, and scholarships.

Home School Association

The availability and make up of these associations vary greatly by state but the basic purpose is to offer resources to home school families. Home School Associations are a great way to build relationships with people who are in a similar situation as you.

Volunteering

There are many opportunities for volunteering. Volunteers are always needed in school and after school. Schools and programs don't always have all the funding they need to be successful. Volunteers offset those costs and free up money that would have been used on staffing, to be used on materials and building costs. You don't have to be an expert in anything to volunteer. You just need to be willing to help. Volunteer opportunities vary greatly. Some common volunteer opportunities are staffing booths at field day, maintenance and beautification at the school, staffing the snack bar at a sporting event, passing out fliers at a recital, creating the school newsletter, directing visitors on which way to go.

School events

Many schools offer things like Parent University nights where parents can learn about programs and how to navigate the school system. Schools also have things like recitals, plays, open house, and art nights. All of these are great events where you can get into the school and meet teachers, administrators, and even your child's friends.

Donations

Parents, who can't always get to the school, can still participate and be known through donations. Most schools need fundraisers to supplement the extra-curricular programs they offer. These fundraisers often come in the form of a catalog. Parents can take those catalogs to work, to their gyms, or to meetings and sell to help the school earn money. This help is greatly appreciated by most schools.

REFLECTIONS:

How do you think staying active in the school benefits your child?

_____

_____

_____

_____

What ways have you been active or can you start to be active in your child's school?

_____

_____

_____

_____

_____

_____

_____

_____

_____

_____

_____

_____

STEP
10

Stay Positive

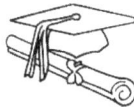

If you don't like something, change it.
If you can't change it, change your attitude.

Stay Positive

This may not seem like a big enough point to dedicate and entire step to, but it definitely is. There will be many difficulties as your family navigates the education system. Your child's personality may change, your family's needs may change, or a school that you were once in love with may change. All of that can lead to struggles and frustration.

However, if you continue to reassess and apply the TEN STEPS in this book, *starting back at #1 when necessary*, you will ensure the best education your child can get.

The *best* education doesn't mean things will be perfect every day or that your student will excel at every class. There will still be difficult teachers to deal with at even a "good" school, but if you've built positive relationships with the school, you will have a better of finding a solution.

It will be a lesson for your child to see that even with the most careful planning, things don't always go exactly as you would hope, but you push through, make the best of it and hold on for a better day.

I define quality education as one where the whole child is being educated. This means your child is being exposed to the world, gaining the tools to navigate it, given a chance to excel, given a chance to be themselves, and being accepted through it all. Your definition of quality education may vary from mine, but no matter what you are, striving for, staying positive throughout the journey will make things much easier to deal with.

Here are some points for how to stay positive as your journey to quality education hits roadblocks and speedways.

Optimism:

Optimism is hopefulness and confidence about the future or the successful outcome of something. Things may not always come together as quickly as you will like. Finding the right education for your child is a journey. Keep reminding yourself that you are capable. Keep your focus on why you are doing what you're doing. This is about your child and in the end; it will all be worth it. When someone tells you *No*, remember that they are not the only one to ask. They are just a simple setback or roadblock. Take a detour if need be. If you keep moving forward, you will eventually get a *Yes* and you will find what you are looking for.

Open Minded:

Being open-minded means having or showing a mind receptive to new ideas or arguments. This is easier said than done. We all have preconceived notions based on experiences. The older we get, the harder it is to break those ideas and become open to new things.

The education system has changed immensely in just the

last decade. Things are moving faster and technology is being embraced more and more. We have to be open to new ways of doing things. Being open doesn't mean we have to blindly accept everything. Just because everyone else is doing it one way doesn't mean that it's the best way for you and your family. Being open simply means you are willing to listen, willing to learn, and willing to think about alternative ways of accomplishing your goals.

At the same time, be open to hearing other views on education. Ask questions to find out why things are done one way over another, maybe it could be positive for your family. Being open increases your families options beyond the scope of what you're used to and may bring opportunities you never expected.

Options:

One great thing to remember is that there are *always* options. Sometimes they're not the exact options you want in the beginning, but if you make the best of things and keep moving forward, more options will come.

If you feel home school would be the best thing for your child, but you don't feel equipped to do it, *Take Charge*. Take classes to sharpen your skills. Read books to expand your knowledge. Use your resources *(Step #4)* to meet people who are home schooling and get advice from them. You may find that most parents felt just as you do when they began their home schooling journey.

If you want to send your child to private school, but don't have the money, *Take Charge*. Get a second job or apply for scholarships and grants. Ask family, friends or community members for advice on making ends meet. You may be surprised to find there are people who are willing to help or can offer resources that could help you.

There are always options, so don't let a roadblock stop you from moving forward in your quest for a quality education for your child!

REFLECTIONS:

How can a positive attitude help your family through the education process?

_____

_____

_____

_____

Other reflections:

_____

_____

_____

_____

_____

_____

_____

_____

_____

_____

_____

_____

_____

_____

Quotes

...and one last thing

If you can't fly, then run. If you can't run, then walk. If you can't walk, then crawl. But whatever you do, keep moving.

...ONE LAST THING

This book was a labor of love for me. I've always shared my thoughts on education with friends and family, but as the years passed, my passion for education has grown.

I believe education is the root of everything. Without it our society will wither and die. We must educate ourselves so we can pass that education and thirst for knowledge on to our children.

When I speak of education, it's not simply reading, writing, and arithmetic; it's education in life in its entirety. The good, the bad, the exciting, and the not so exciting parts of life must be taught to prepare children how to become productive citizens.

Education goes beyond a school building or even a book. Education is happening every day, all around us. We can learn from our interactions with others, from a simple bird gliding through the sky, or from a little baby just opening her eyes for the first time.

Education never stops, but we must be open to it, we must teach our children to look for it and crave it. They need knowledge of who we are as a society, how we got where we are, and how we can continue to grow and change for the better. Real education teaches us how to think for ourselves, how to seek out information, and how to give back to the world in a positive way.

It's my hope that this book helps you find the quality education for your child that will nurture their desire for knowledge.

We have a powerful potential in our youth and we must have the courage to change old ideas and practices so that we may direct their power toward good ends.
-Dr. Mary McLeod Bethune

QUOTES

Here are just a few quotes that have inspired me throughout my journey. I hope they help you as much as they have helped me.

STEP 1
There's nothing more beautiful than acceptance for who you truly are - Unknown

STEP 2
Intelligence plus character - that is the goal of true education. - Dr. Martin Luther King, Jr.

STEP 3
If a child can't learn the way we teach, maybe we should teach the way they learn – Ignacio Estrada

STEP 4
Don't sit and wait for opportunities to come. Get up and make them – Madam CJ Walker

STEP 5
Coming together is the beginning. Keeping together is progress. Working together is success. – Henry Ford

STEP 6
I've learned that I still have a lot to learn – Dr. Maya Angelou

STEP 7
A child educated only at school, is an uneducated child –
George Satayana

STEP 8
I can accept failure - everyone fails at something. But I can't accept not trying. – Michael Jordan

STEP 9
Nothing will work, unless you do – Dr. Maya Angelou

STEP 10
If you don't like something, change it. If you can't change it, change your attitude. – Dr. Maya Angelou

Knowledge is the prime need of the hour – Dr. Mary Mcleod Bethune

From the first, I made my learning, what little it was, useful in every way I could – Dr. Mary McLeod Bethune

Education is the most powerful weapon, which you can use to change the world. – Nelson Mandela

Education is the key to unlock the golden door of freedom – George Washington Carver

Excellence is not an act but a habit. The things you do the most are the things you will do the best. – Marva Collins

There is no greater agony than bearing an untold story inside you – Dr. Maya Angelou

There is a brilliant child locked inside every student. – Marva Collins

I can always look through the muddy waters and see dry ground – Modjeska Simkins

We may encounter many defeats in our lives, but we must never be defeated. – Dr. Maya Angelou

If you really want to accomplish something, you'll find a way. If you don't, you'll find an excuse. – Jim Rohn

Success doesn't come to you, you go to it. – Marva Collins

If you can't fly, then run. If you can't run, then walk. If you can't walk, then crawl. But whatever you do, keep moving. – Dr. Martin Luther King, Jr.

The mediocre teacher tells. The good teacher explains. The superior teacher demonstrates. The great teacher inspires. - William Arthur Ward

The only real mistake is the one from which we learn nothing. – Henry Ford

Fair doesn't mean giving every child the same thing, it means giving every child what they need. – Rick Lavoie

I'm not telling you it's going to be easy. I'm telling you it's going to be worth it. – Art Williams

The best teachers are those who show you where to look, but don't tell you what to see. – Alexandra K. Trenfor

Hold fast to dreams for if dreams die. Life is a broken winged bird that cannot fly – Langton Hughes

We have a powerful potential in our youth and we must have the courage to change old ideas and practices so that we may direct their power toward good ends –
Dr. Mary McLeod Bethune

Additional Resources

www.schooldigger.com
www.powerschool.net
www.greatschools.org
www.pta.org
www.pto.org

www.ingramcontent.com/pod-product-compliance
Lightning Source LLC
Chambersburg PA
CBHW071559040426
42452CB00008B/1230